ED EMBERLEY'S
FINGERPRINT
Drawing Book

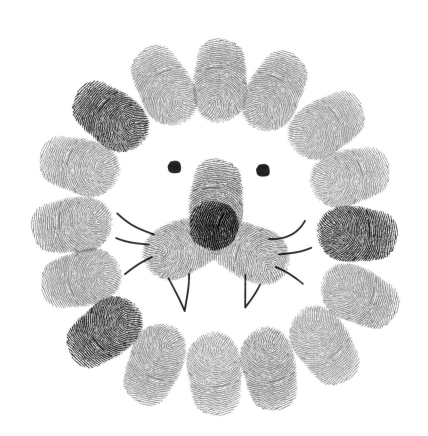

 LITTLE, BROWN AND COMPANY

New York ✧ Boston ✧ London

This book shows how to make pictures using your fingerprints and a few scribbles, dots, and lines....

This row shows what to draw. 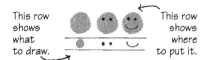 This row shows where to put it.

Simple step-by-step instructions show you how.

 1. Press ink. 2. Press paper. 3. Draw.

ABOUT PRINTERS

Your finger will do for a start.

For cleaner hands and a greater choice of sizes you can make your own stampers.

An artist's gum-rubber eraser is easy to carve and fun to use.

So are assorted veggies such as carrots or potatoes.

For a very special gift, for yourself or someone else, you can have a custom rubber stamp made from your fingerprint. Inquire at any printer or office-supply store.

ABOUT INK PADS

There are a number of different kinds of ink pads you can use. Office stamp pads are inexpensive and can be found in places that sell office supplies. Colors are limited to red, blue, black, and sometimes green.

CAUTION: Since pads are made for adult office use, the ink is not necessarily nontoxic or washable.

Craft stamp pads are harder to find and usually more expensive than standard office ink pads. They can be found in many places that sell arts and crafts supplies. They come in lots of bright colors and are available washable and nontoxic.

You could also try making your own ink pads from cloth or paper towels and whatever coloring you have on hand. This is the least expensive way to go, but it will take some experimentation to get just the right combination of paint and pad.

Of course, you are not limited to stamping or printing. Cut paper, fabric, stencils, blobs of paint, lumps of clay—anything with which you can make a roundish shape will work using these instructions.

ABOUT MARKERS

A pencil will do for a s

After that, which ma you choose will depe the size of your prin the ink used.

For this book I used colored pencil for th colored lines and a f point fiber-tip pen fo black lines. Both wer found in the statione section of my local drugstore.

ODDS AND EN

You will also need pap print on and a table work on; plastic or newspapers to protec table; work clothes t protect the artist; a paper towels and soa water for cleaning up

are billions of fingerprints in the world.
o have ever been found that are just alike.
never has been and there never will be fingerprints just like yours.
makes your fingerprints very special.

THIS AND THAT
CIRCLES AND OVALS

ed two kinds of fingerprints
make this book. Ovals and
les.

ovals were made by using my
le fingertip.

circles were made by using
the very tip of my finger.

carrot
ting, use a
aight cut
circles, and
angled cut
ovals.

—Adult supervision is advised
for ALL cutting.

ONE OR MANY

Sometimes when I
make fingerprint
pictures, I like to use
just one color
at a time because
it's quick and easy.

Sometimes I use lots of colors and lots
of fingers.

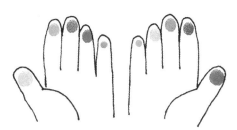

When I want to change colors, I dip my
finger in a glass of water and then wipe
it off on a stack of paper towels.
That keeps my ink pads bright and clean.

Rinse.   Wipe.

EXTRA FOR EXPERTS
HALF PRINTS

In a few places in this book, I used half prints.
Here's how I made them.

1. Place paper   2. Print half   3. Remove   4. Draw.
   shield.   on, half off   paper
                     paper shield.   shield.

1. Print.   2. Cover with   3. Print half on,
                     paper shield.   half off paper
                                       shield.

4. Remove paper shield.   5. Draw.   Too complicated?
                                       Use just one color.

Half circles are just right for making water-
melons, monkeys, and other things. Can you
find the half prints in these two things?

THE GARDEN

FLOWER

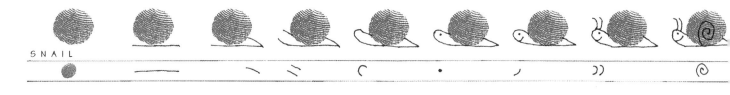

SNAIL

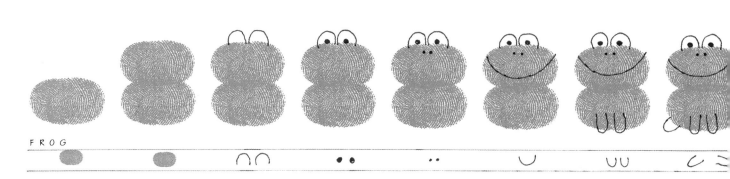

FROG

ALL FLOWER

CROCUS

TULIP

OWN ANT

CATERPILLAR

CENTIPEDE

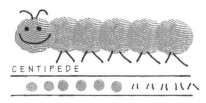

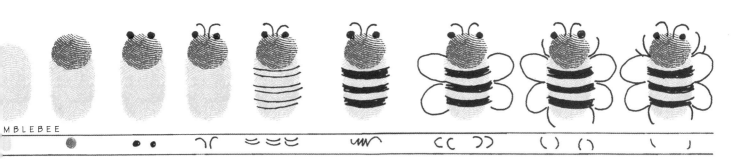

MBLEBEE

THE POND

TURTLE

DUCK

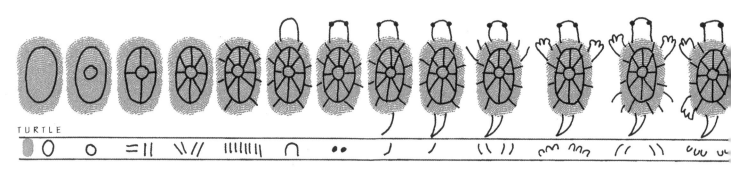

POLLYWOG

BUTTERFLY

MING FROG

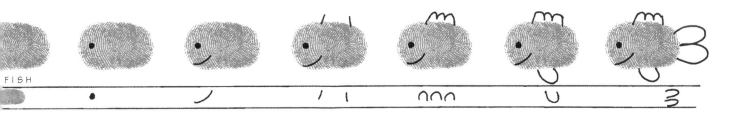

FISH

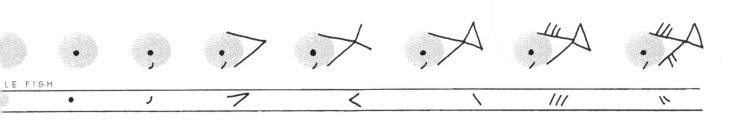

LE FISH

FINGERLINGS

I ALSO CALL THESE MY
TEENY TINIES. I USE A
DIFFERENT FINGERTIP FOR
EACH COLOR.

SPRING

SUMME

RABBIT

MOUSE

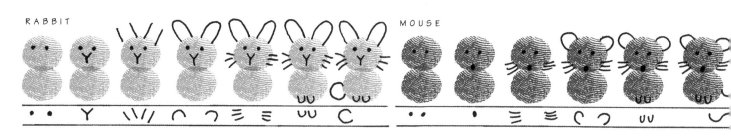

OWL

FROG

DOG

BEAVER

FALL

FALL

WINTER

TTING CAT

BIRD

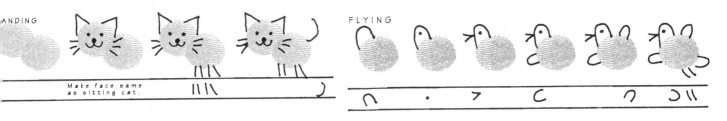

ANDING

Make face same
as sitting cat.

FLYING

NNING

Make face same
as sitting cat.

PECKING

ANIMALS

ELEPHANT

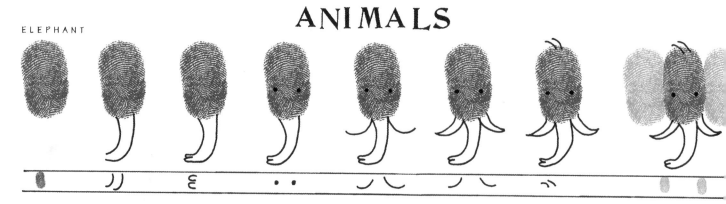

BABY ELEPHANT

LION

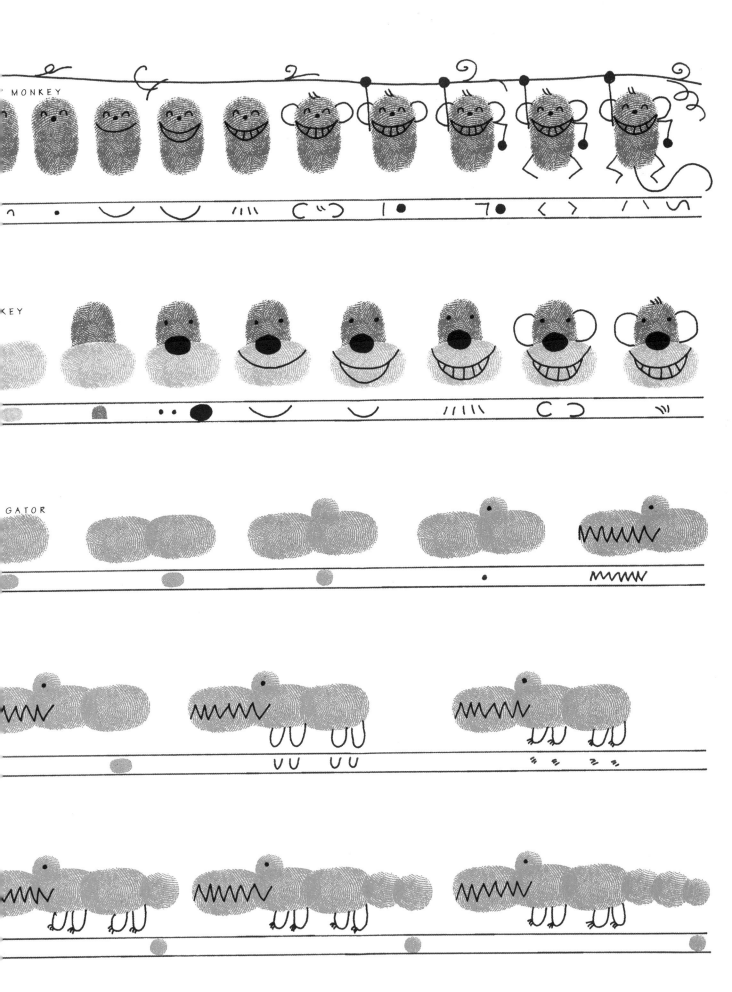

MONKEY

KEY

GATOR

MORE ANIMALS

RACCOON

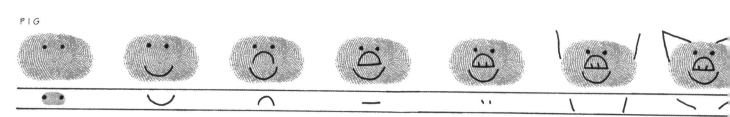

PIG

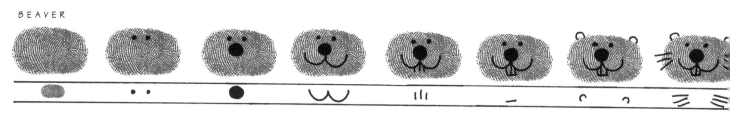

BEAVER

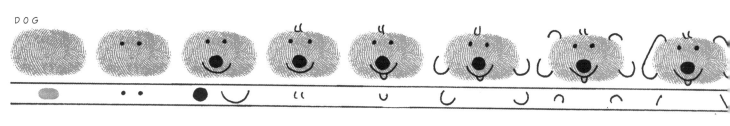

DOG

CAT

SMALL BULLDOG

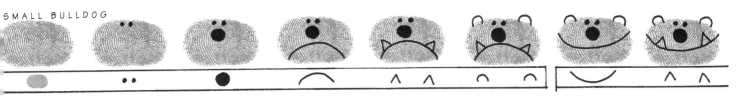

MOUSE

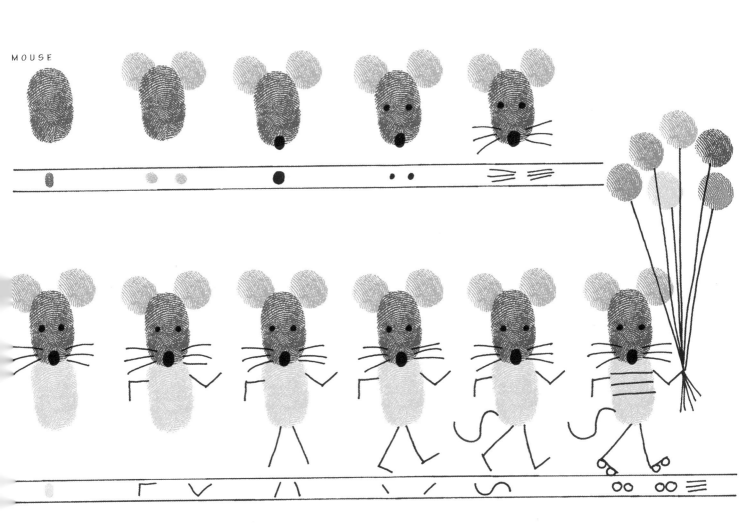

IG BULLDOG

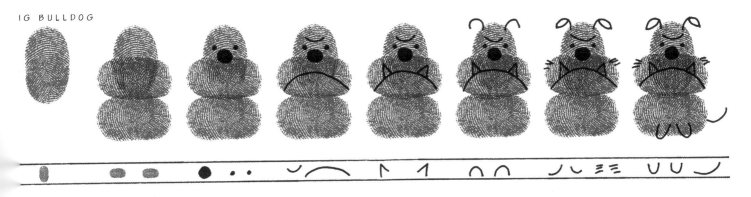

BIRDS

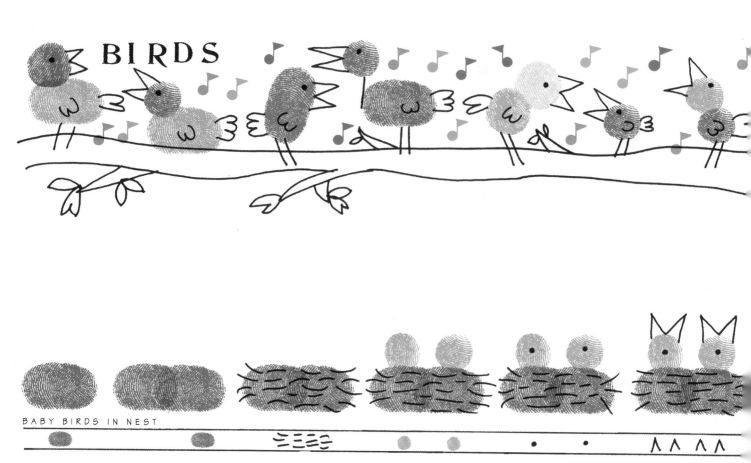

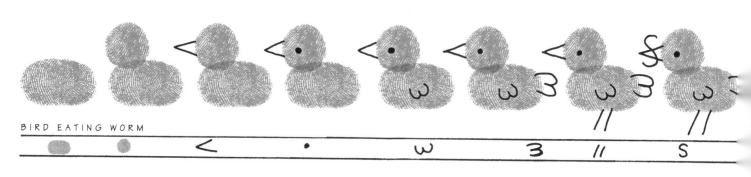

BABY BIRDS IN NEST

BIRD EATING WORM

BIRD FRONT VIEW

BIRD BACK VIEW

D FLYING

D SINGING

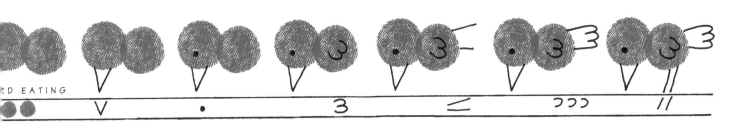

RD EATING

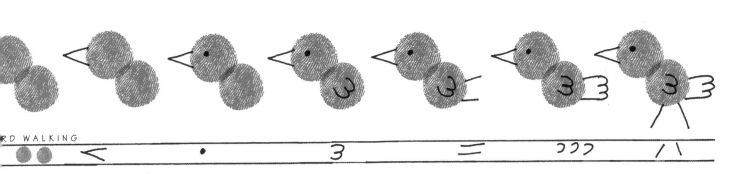

RD WALKING

BEAN BUDDIES

I THINK FINGERPRINTS LOOK LIKE LITTLE BEANS. I LIKE TO USE THESE LITTLE "FINGER BEANS" TO MAKE ALL DIFFERENT KINDS OF LITTLE BEAN BUDDIES.

BASIC

PEA BEAN BUDDY   BAKED BEAN BUDDY   LIMA BEAN BUDDY   JELLY BEAN BUDDY

SPEAKING

HI!

POINTING

LOOK

(LOOK

YAWNING

HO HUM

HO HUM

CELEBRATING

HOORA

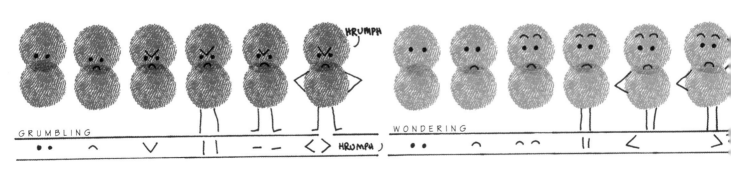

GRUMBLING

HRUMPH

HRUMPH

WONDERING

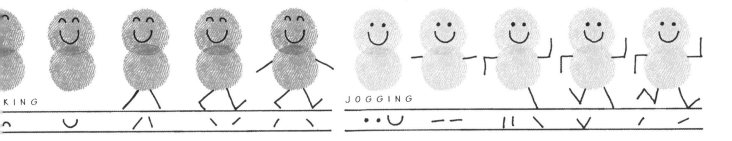

KING

JOGGING

NING

WINNING

LET

HULA

CING

TAP DANCING

LITTLE CLOWN

NAPOLEON

SAILOR

QUEEN

KING

PRINCE

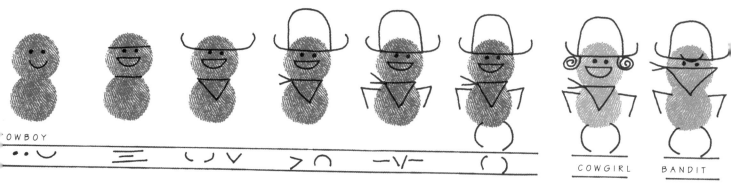

COWBOY

COWGIRL   BANDIT

PIRATE

SUPERPERSON

EVIL VILLAIN

19

   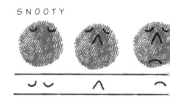

FEELINGS

HAPPY

VERY HAPPY

VERY VERY HAPPY

SNOOTY

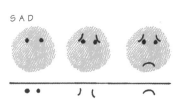 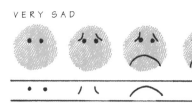 

SAD

VERY SAD

VERY VERY SAD

 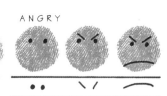  

UPSET

ANGRY

VERY ANGRY

VERY VERY ANGRY

 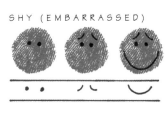 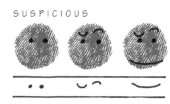 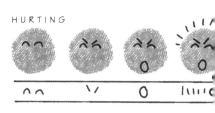

SLY (MISCHIEVOUS)

SHY (EMBARRASSED)

SUSPICIOUS

HURTING

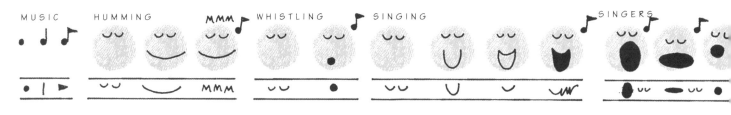

MUSIC **HUMMING** **WHISTLING** **SINGING** **SINGERS**

20

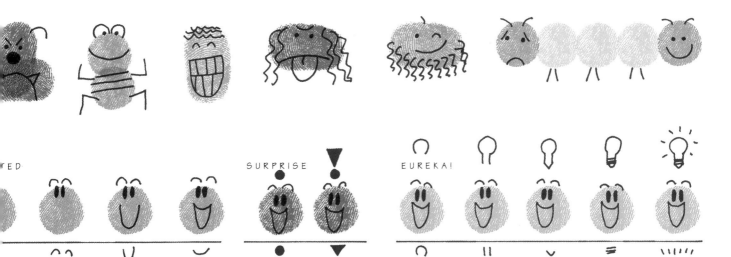

ED

SURPRISE

EUREKA!

LED

IN LOVE

BOP!

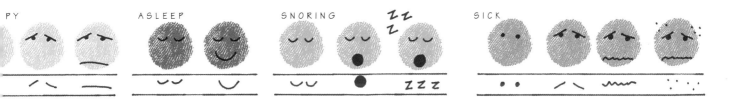

PY

ASLEEP

SNORING

SICK

HOT

HELP!

RY

YUM
YUM

YUKI

PHOOEY!

SKIPPING ROPE

BICYCLING

SKATEBOARDING

ROLLER-SKATING

22

SUMMER FUN

CHASING BUTTERFLIES

SWIMMING

SURFING

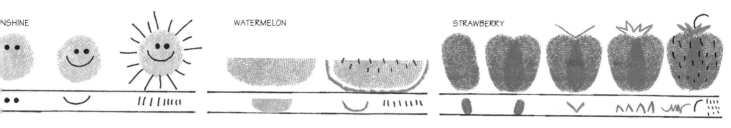

SUNSHINE
WATERMELON
STRAWBERRY

LAWN
MOWING

SUNBATHING

BASEBALL

FALL FUN

APPLE

PEAR

YELLOW APPLE

HAPPY GREEN APPLE

GRAPES

FARMING

LACROSSE

SOCCER

CHEERLEADER

WINTER ☐ FUN

PENGUIN FRONT VIEW

PENGUIN SIDE VIEW

SNOWPERSON

⌐ ○ •• ⌣ / ‖ ○○ ≫ ╱╱ ♩♩

⊗ ⊗ •• ⌣ ╲ ╱ ╱ │ ⌐ ⌐ │ — ww

•• ○ ∪ ⌣ — │ ‖ ∨ ≥ │ — ∟ ∪ ⌐ ─ │ ─ ♫ ●

HOLIDAYS

EASTER BUNNY

EASTER EGG

CHOCOLATE EGG

CHICK

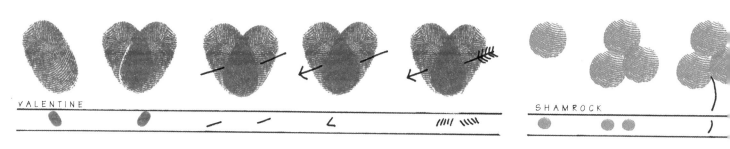

VALENTINE

SHAMROCK

LEPRECHAUN

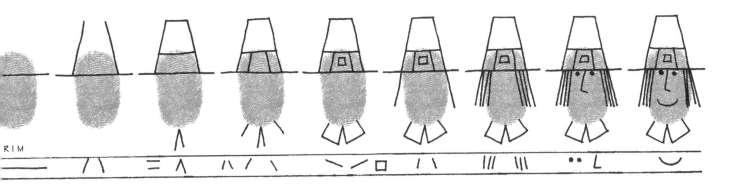

HALLOWEEN

WITCH

BAT

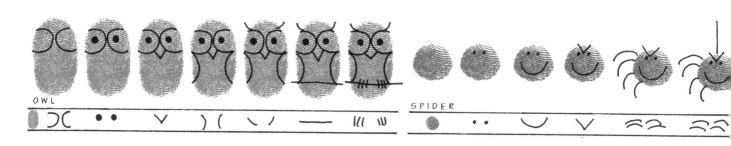

OWL

SPIDER

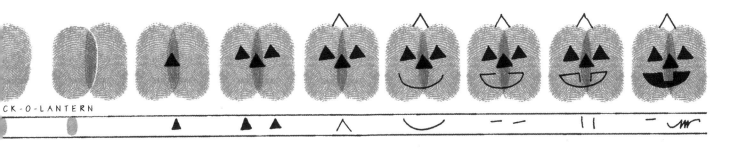

CK-O-LANTERN

ING WITCH

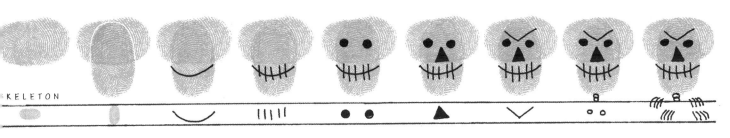

KELETON

AT

HO HO HO HO HO HO

JINGLE

JINGLE

JINGLE

JINGLE

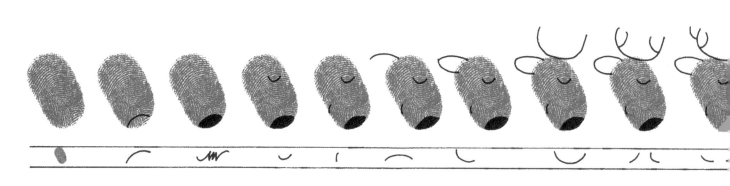

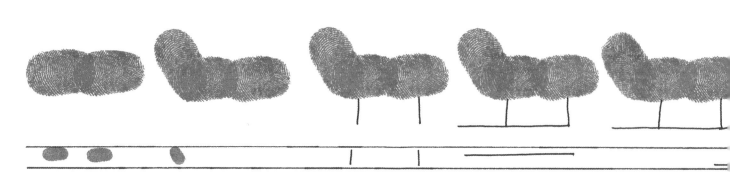

COMET * CUPID * DONNER * BLITZEN*

JINGLE JINGLE JINGLE

LAND SEA AND AIR

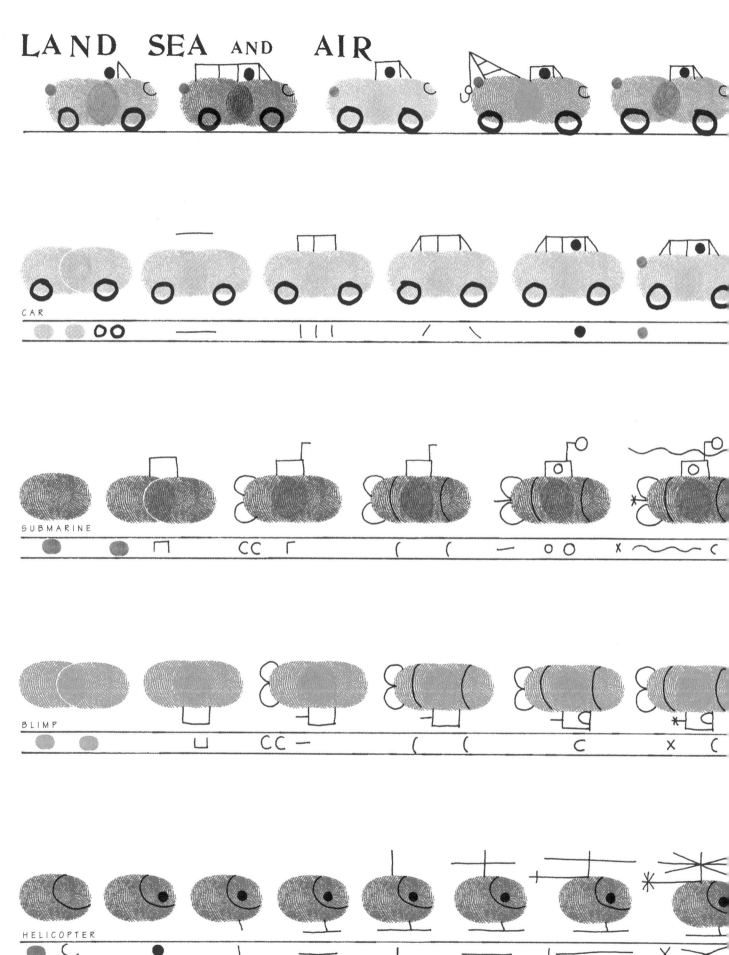

CAR

SUBMARINE

BLIMP

HELICOPTER

TRAIN

INE

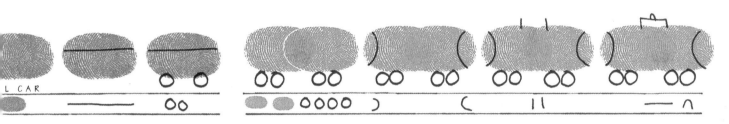

L CAR

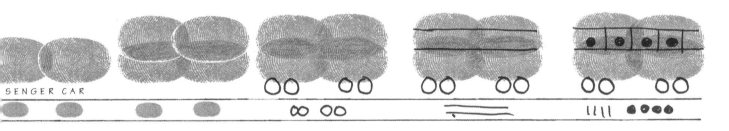

SENGER CAR

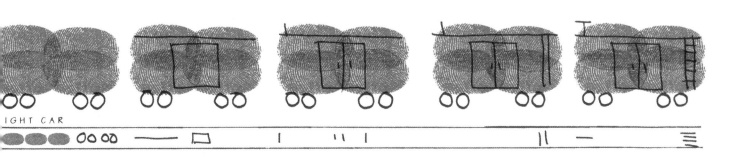

IGHT CAR

RAINBOW CLOWN

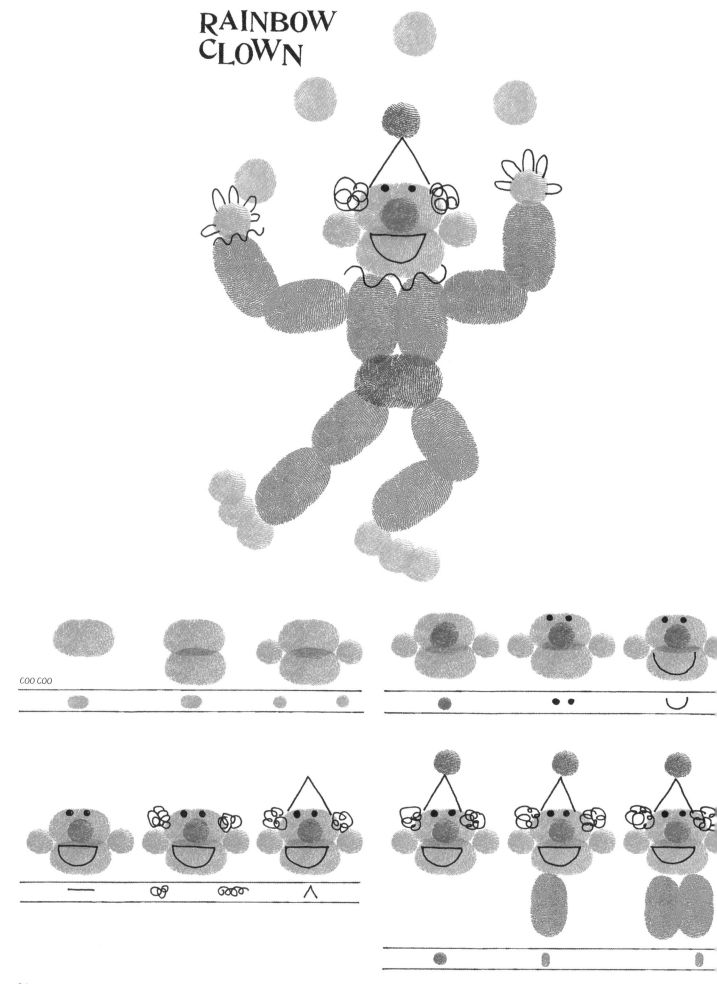

COO COO

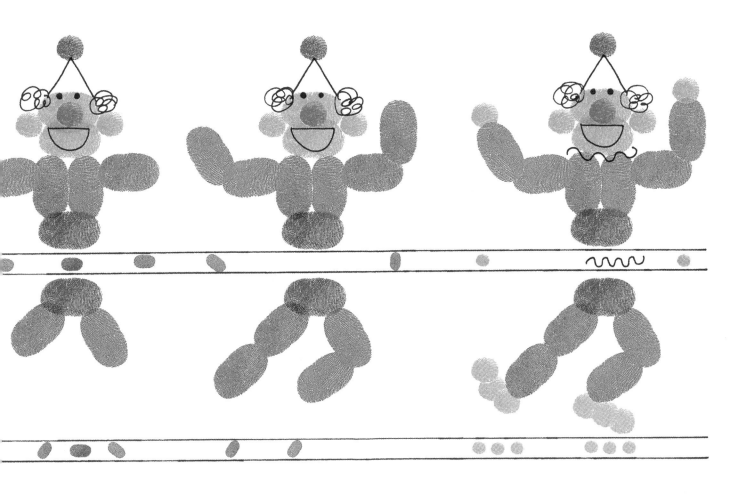

TER

LULU

RAINBOW DRAGON

LION

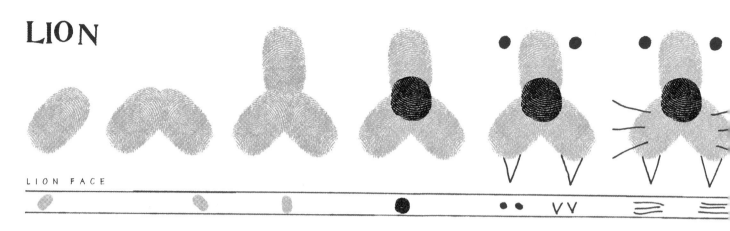

LION FACE

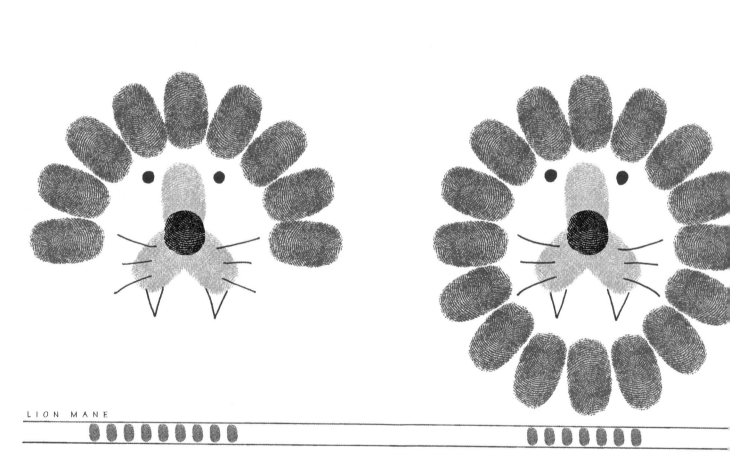

LION MANE

RAINBOW
LIONS

SKETCH BOOK

HERE ARE SOME FINGERPRINT THINGS I COULD NOT FIT INTO THIS BOOK. CAN YOU FIGURE OUT HOW I MADE THEM?

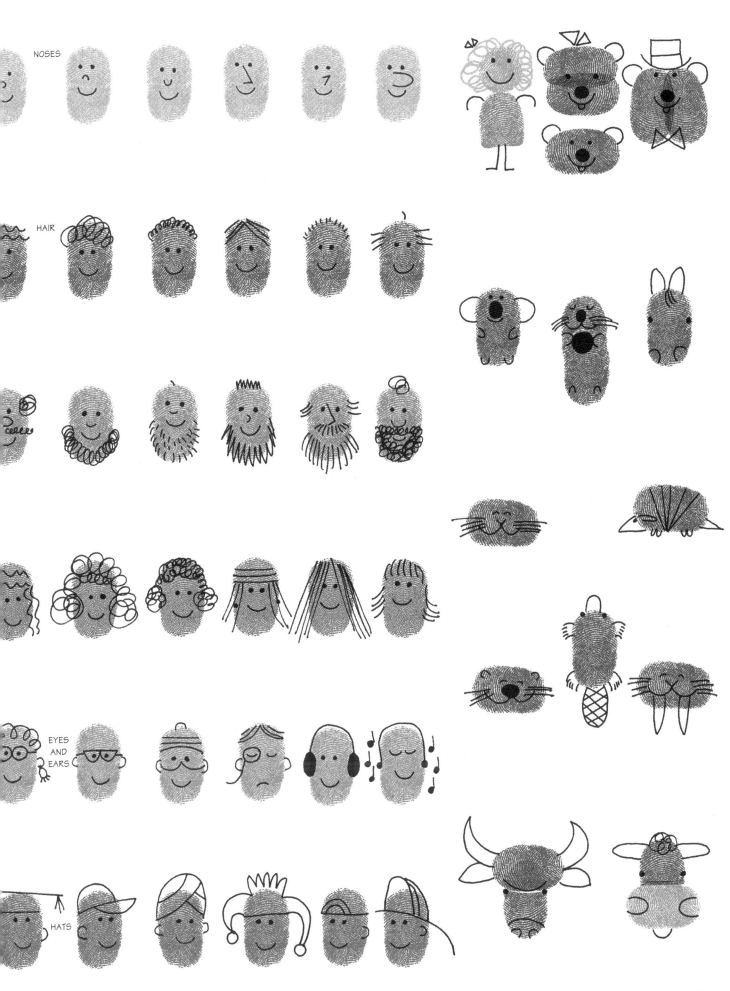

NOSES

HAIR

EYES
AND
EARS

HATS

ADVANCED FINGER-PRINTING

FOR THE ADVENTUROUS—
JUST A FEW OTHER WAYS TO COMBINE PRINTS,
COLORS, SIMPLE LINES, AND SOME
IMAGINATION TO MAKE PICTURES.
THERE ARE LOTS LEFT FOR YOU TO DISCOVER.
HAPPY DISCOVERING!

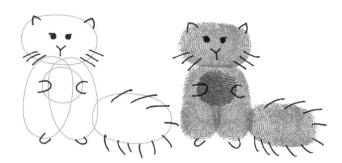

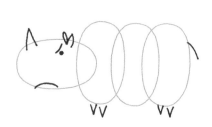

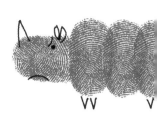

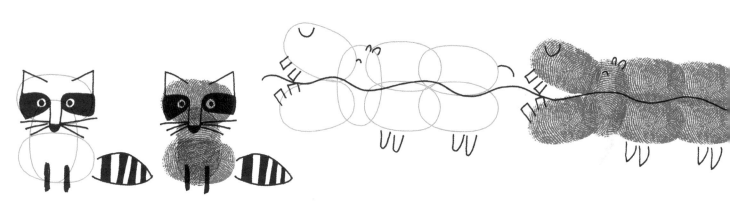

SOMETHING VERY SPECIAL

The instructions in this book are meant to show a few ways to turn fingerprints into an owl or a cat or a dog, etc. Much has been left for you to explore and discover.

Just as no two fingerprints will ever look just alike, no two fingerprint pictures will ever look just alike. Fingerprints will be lighter or darker, lines will be thicker or thinner, colors will be different.

That means no other fingerprint pictures will look just like the ones in this book, or just like yours. That's what will make your pictures "something very special."

This is the way this book shows you how to make a fingerprint owl.

Here are some other "explorations."

Sometimes I like to use natural colors, sometimes I like to use imaginary colors.

Sometimes I like to use other fingerprints.

Sometimes I like to add a few extra lines.

Little, Brown and Company

Hachette Book Group USA

1271 Avenue of the Americas, New York, NY 10020

Visit our Web site at www.lb-kids.com

First Revised Paperback Edition 2005

10 9 8 7 6 5 4 3

WKT

Printed in China

Library of Congress Cataloging-in-Publication Data

Emberley, Ed.

[Fingerprint drawing book]

Ed Emberley's fingerprint drawing book—1st ed.

p. cm.

ISBN 0-316-78969-0

1. Fingerprints in art. 2. Drawing—Technique. 1. Title.

NC825.F55 E46 2001

741.2—dc21

00-031026